LIVING DANGEROUSLY

PILOTS

127415

LINDSAY PEACOCK

GEC **GARRETT EDUCATIONAL CORPORATION**

LIVING **DANGEROUSLY**

ASTRONAUTS
DIVERS
FIREFIGHTERS
PILOTS
RACING DRIVERS
STUNT PERFORMERS

Series Editor: James Kerr
Designer: Helen White

Cover: A Tornado "reaches for the sky."

Edited by Rebecca Stefoff

Library of Congress Cataloging-in-Publication Data

Peacock, Lindsay T.
    Pilots/Lindsay Peacock.
        p. cm.—(Living dangerously)
    Includes index.
    Summary: Briefly points out some of the risks faced by different
kinds of pilots.
    ISBN 1-56074-040-X
    1. Air pilots—Juvenile literature. 2. Test pilots—Juvenile
literature. 3. Air pilots, Military—Juvenile literature.
4. Hazardous occupations—Juvenile literature. [1. Air pilots.]
I. Title II. Series.
TL547.P36 1992b
629.13'092—dc20
                                          91-39097
                                              CIP
                                              AC1

CONTENTS

THE PILOT'S JOB

What exactly does a pilot do? In the very simplest of terms, he or she is responsible for getting a flying machine – whether it be an airplane or a helicopter, or even an airship or a balloon – to travel safely between two points. It sounds easy, doesn't it? But, like many jobs, it has its share of danger, for the sky can be a very risky place indeed. Even the smallest mistake can have serious results.

LEFT AND ABOVE Fire is one of the greatest dangers that pilots face. This is a practice drill for firefighters.

Different types of flying have different levels of risk. Airliner pilots, for instance, face fewer hazards than most military pilots. This is because airliners, like the massive Boeing 747 and the Airbus, usually travel directly from one location to another. During a typical journey, an airliner will spend much of the time cruising at high altitude. This gives pilots more time to think about any problems that might occur, and more time to decide what to do if something does go wrong.

In contrast, many military pilots spend a lot of time flying low and fast, as they try to improve their skills in the delivery of weapons such as bombs. These flights also involve a good deal of maneuvering, with aircraft twisting and turning this way and that as they flash across the countryside. By regularly practicing this kind of flight, military pilots have a better chance of surviving if they ever have to go to war. Staying close to the ground and using hills and valleys for cover helps limit the risk of being shot down by enemy defenses such as missiles.

ABOVE **Formation flying is just one skill that military pilots must learn.**

RIGHT **An F-16 pilot puts his aircraft into a right-hand turn at high altitude.**

Flying low and fast is very exciting. It is also dangerous. If something goes wrong when flying at 75 yards above the ground and close to 500 miles per hour (mph), a pilot has only a few brief moments to decide what the problem is. But, despite all the dangers, there are many who choose to fly military jet fighters such as the American F-16 Fighting Falcon and the European Tornado.

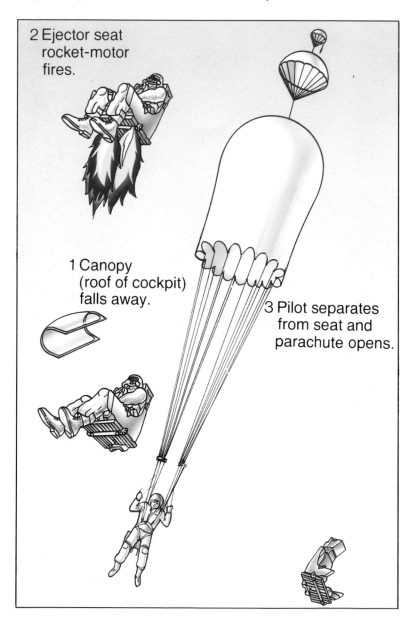

2 Ejector seat rocket-motor fires.

1 Canopy (roof of cockpit) falls away.

3 Pilot separates from seat and parachute opens.

Fast-jet aircrew are able to use ejector seats if they have to leave their aircraft in an emergency.

Strike aircraft like the British Buccaneer spend a lot of time at low level.

Why is that? Job satisfaction must be a big factor. Flying a sleek and deadly warplane low and fast offers a real challenge to many pilots.

Airline pilots may well face fewer challenges but they do gain other rewards — money is one. The job of an airline captain is very well paid. It is also seen by many as being an exciting job. However, the glamour of overseas travel may disguise the often routine nature of the work.

Other types of civil flying are less well paid. Some of these involve dangers that even the military fast-jet pilot would think twice about. Aerial crop-dusting is one such job. To fly a single-engined light aircraft at ultra-low level – between 3 and 6 yards above the ground – the spray pilot must be a master of precision. The chemicals the pilot has to spray are costly, and waste is not looked upon kindly by those who pay for the pilot's services.

Like the military pilot, the spray pilot has little margin for error. Even a minor lapse of concentration can result in catastrophe. So, too, can mechanical problems such as engine failure. A sudden loss of power will give a pilot little option but to try for a hasty forced landing. Once again, though, it is possible to gain immense job satisfaction as a spray pilot.

Crop-spraying in Louisiana.

RIGHT **The cockpit or "front office" is a cramped and uncomfortable place with plenty to keep the pilot occupied.**
1   **Head-up display (covered)**
2   **Instruments and control switches**
3   **Radio equipment**
4   **Rudder pedals**
5   **Control column (controls movement of the aircraft)**

BECOMING **A PILOT**

6 **Throttle levers**
7 **Map locker**
8 **Radar display**
9 **Undercarriage lever (controls landing gear)**
10 **Cockpit canopy framing**

How does someone learn to fly and become a pilot? There are a number of ways. Although these differ slightly from country to country, the basic rules are the same and always lead to a novice pilot's going "solo." This means flying a circuit of the airfield completely unaccompanied, after about ten hours of instruction.

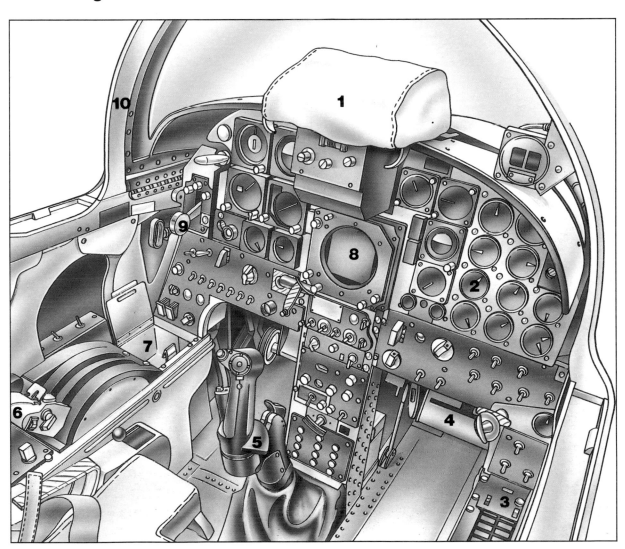

A successful "solo" flight is an important milestone in any pilot's career, and is almost always a cause for celebration. However, it is just the first hurdle to be cleared, and there are other tasks that must be mastered before the student is allowed to venture further afield. Throughout this important learning period, the student pilot must also display a good deal of commitment and discipline if he or she is to succeed.

Perhaps the easiest way of becoming a pilot is to go to a civil flying school and study for the private pilot's license (PPL). To earn this, a student has to learn all of the basic skills needed to fly a small single-engined aircraft safely by day in good weather. Only when the student has mastered these skills, has satisfied the instructor by flying "solo," and has passed written and practical examinations as well as a tough medical check-up, is a pilot's license granted.

After that, it is possible to move on to more advanced aspects of flying, like piloting a multi-engined aircraft in poor weather or by night. This is done with the aid of special instruments that show whether the aircraft is flying straight and level, or whether it is climbing, turning, or diving. Success in these more advanced challenges results in an instrument "rating." Students can continue to gain other "ratings" that in theory will eventually allow them to fly airliners.

In practice, however, most airlines prefer to recruit pilots directly from the military or

British Royal Air Force pilots now receive much of their training in the turboprop Tucano.

to run their own specialized training schools. Entry to these schools is open to anybody with the correct qualifications. However, the competition for places is intense. Only the very best candidates are selected, because the training of airline pilots is a very expensive process.

Pilots can also learn to fly with the military. Again, this is a costly business, so early lessons are usually given on a light aircraft that is relatively inexpensive to operate. In the British Royal Air Force, this initial training is done on an aircraft called the Chipmunk. Later, the new pilots move on to more advanced aircraft, such as the propeller-driven Tucano and the jet-powered Hawk. It is in such aircraft that they will learn to master other skills such as formation flying, aerobatics, gunnery, battle tactics, and weapons delivery.

ABOVE Most modern warplanes are able to carry air-to-air missiles to destroy other fighters.

LEFT Some military flight groups are masters at the art of formation display aerobatics.

Eventually, they will be introduced to the types of aircraft that they will fly when they join a front-line squadron. This period of training is perhaps the hardest test of all, because the aircraft are almost certain to be much more complicated than anything they have flown before.

Although some of the latest generation of interceptors are single-seaters, most modern strike fighters, like Europe's Tornado and America's F-15E Strike Eagle, need a two-person crew if they are to be operated to full potential. Computers can help with tasks such as navigation and weapons release, but the workload is felt to be just too great for one individual. That is why it is necessary to provide a navigator or weapons systems operator to assist the pilot.

THE TEST PILOT

Like most things connected with flying, the job of the test pilot has changed greatly in recent times. This is due mainly to modern computers. These are able to predict how a new aircraft will fly long before it takes to the sky for the first time. In addition, much use is made of flight simulators. These are machines that are able to give a test pilot a good idea of what to expect when flying a new and unproven aircraft.

A modern-day pilot's uniform.

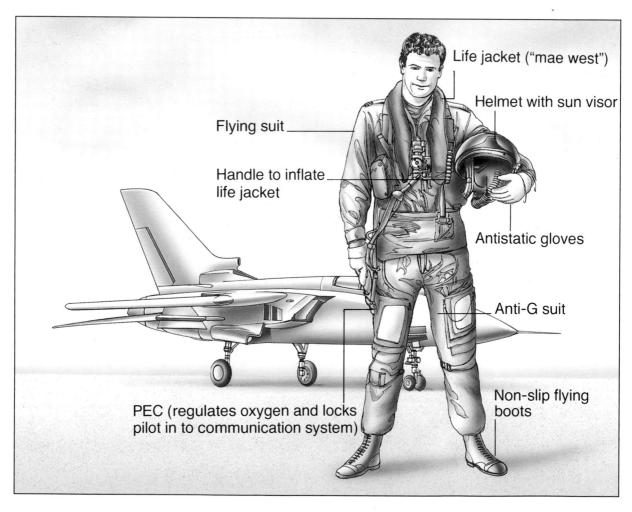

Life jacket ("mae west")

Helmet with sun visor

Flying suit

Handle to inflate life jacket

Antistatic gloves

Anti-G suit

Non-slip flying boots

PEC (regulates oxygen and locks pilot in to communication system)

The B-2 "stealth" bomber takes off for the first time at the start of a long test program.

As a result, the job of the test pilot is now far less dangerous, as many risks have been eliminated before an aircraft flies for the first time. Even though it is much safer these days, being a test pilot is still seen as a glamorous and exciting job. In reality, much of the test pilot's work is routine and unexciting, but it is still a rewarding occupation and can sometimes be a terrifying one.

Today's test pilot must also be far more knowledgeable than in the past. He or she must obviously be a capable pilot. By itself, though, flying skill is not enough, for it is also essential to have a good knowledge of engineering and the laws of aerodynamics. This is because the modern test pilot is just one member of a team. This team also includes designers, engineers, and computer operators. Together they have the job of ensuring that aircraft are as safe as they can be, whether they are intended for military or civilian service.

The YF-22 is one of the latest American fighters.

Almost 50 years ago, at the dawn of the jet age, the job of a test pilot was less complex. It was also much more dangerous. Many pilots were killed flying from test bases around the world as they sought to expand our knowledge of flight. Perhaps the best known of these bases is the US Air Force flight test center at Edwards Air Force Base in California. It is there that the newest warplanes – planes like the B-2 "stealth" bomber and the very latest YF-22 and YF-23 fighters – are tested.

It was also from there that the American test pilot Charles "Chuck" Yeager flew when he broke the sound barrier and exceeded Mach One for the very first time in the Bell X-1 rocket plane in October, 1947. It was a most courageous act, for there were many who said it was impossible and that he would be killed in the attempt. Despite that, he went ahead, made history, and lived to tell the tale.

Others were less fortunate. At Edwards and a score of other locations, many fine pilots lost their lives as they flew ever faster and ever higher. Reaching out to the fringes of space, some of these pilots paved the way for the astronauts and cosmonauts who came later. In experimental craft such as the North American X-15, the pilots Scott Crossfield, Mike Adams, and Neil Armstrong (later the first person to set foot on the moon) were carried beneath a special B-52 Stratofortress "mother ship." Dropped from the "mother ship" at high altitude, they lit the X-15's powerful rocket motors and blazed a fiery trail into the sky.

In the process, they set records for winged aircraft that have still to be broken,

Pilots associated with the X-15 project pose with one of the three aircraft built.

climbing 67 miles high in August, 1963, and achieving an incredible 4,500 mph in October, 1967. Triumph went hand in hand with tragedy, though, for two of the three X-15s suffered serious accidents, one of which claimed the life of Mike Adams.

Whether engaged in test or service flying, today's fast-jet pilot works in a cramped and uncomfortable environment.

Danger Facts

- At high altitude, pilots must wear bulky pressure-suits if they are to survive in the thin atmosphere.

- Excessive G-force, which might be encountered when testing fighter aircraft, can cause unconsciousness.

- At the 1952 Farnborough air show in England, test pilot John Derry and twenty-eight spectators were killed when the de Havilland DH110 Derry was flying broke up in midair.

FLYING FIREFIGHTERS

Specially built to fight fire from the air, the Canadair CL-215 is used around the world.

When it comes to dangerous flying jobs, there are few that pose quite as many risks as those faced by airborne firefighters. Although some newer aircraft are now used, lots of "water-bombers" are elderly machines that have been specially converted for this job. Many of them are almost 40 years old, and a few date back as far as the Second World War (1939–1945).

Whatever type of airplane they fly, these firefighting pilots earn their money the hard way. Summer months are usually the high-risk periods, when massive forest fires are most likely to break out. Therefore, many firefighting pilots have to travel the world in search of work.

Wherever firefighters work, the risks they face are the same. So are the methods that they use to battle fires from the sky. As they roar over the heart of a fire, they drop the fire-quenching materials – usually water – that are contained in large tanks in the aircraft's belly. Some aircraft have to fly to a nearby airport to reload. Others are able to land on water to refill their tanks: some can do this by skimming across the surface of a lake. Scoops under the plane are extended to gather up water. By collecting water in this way, the planes are able to return quickly to the scene of the fire and drop another load.

A Canadair CL-215 skims across a lake to refill its tanks.

Watching "water-bombers" at work is an impressive sight but it can disguise the dangers that the pilots face. Dropping a load on the right spot calls for pin-point flying. This is often far from easy, because forest fires can produce thick clouds of smoke that obscure vision and increase the risk of flying into the ground.

The air also becomes dangerously overheated. This usually causes severe turbulence, resulting in a very bumpy ride, so it is not a job for those with weak stomachs. In heavy turbulence, great physical strength is called for as the pilot tries to fly the precise pattern needed for accurate delivery.

Work periods can also be long. Even though there are limits on the time that a

Water pours from a CL-215 as it tackles a major fire in southern France.

pilot is allowed to spend on duty, aircrew
are seldom able to give up until the battle is
nearly won and firefighters on the ground
can cope with the fire.

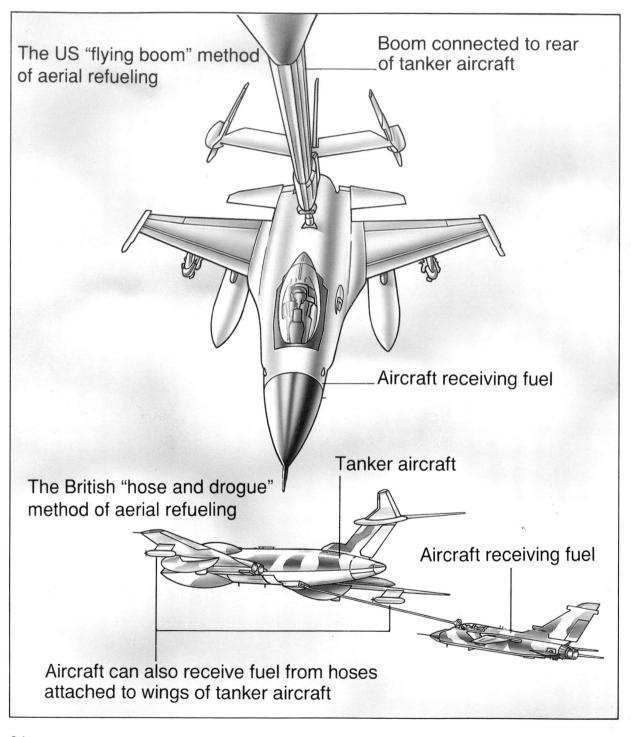

The US "flying boom" method
of aerial refueling

Boom connected to rear
of tanker aircraft

Aircraft receiving fuel

Tanker aircraft

The British "hose and drogue"
method of aerial refueling

Aircraft receiving fuel

Aircraft can also receive fuel from hoses
attached to wings of tanker aircraft

FLYING **AT SEA**

Most of the 80 aircraft on board are visible in this view of an American supercarrier.

LEFT **Aerial refueling – like aerial firefighting – involves precise flying. It is necessary on long military flights.**

In times of peace, perhaps the most dangerous military flying job of all is that of a naval fighter pilot. Apart from the danger involved in flying over the world's oceans and seas, far from the safety of land, there are many other hazards to be faced. For a start, the naval pilot has to learn how to take off from and land on an aircraft carrier at all hours of the day or night, and in all kinds of weather conditions.

Take-off is perhaps less risky, for it is done with the aid of an enormously powerful steam catapult. A big carrier like the nuclear-powered USS *Nimitz* has four of these catapults. Between them, they can launch twenty-four aircraft in just five minutes. During a mass launch, the activity on the huge flight deck becomes frantic as aircraft move in quick succession to the catapults. Once there, pilots select full power and are then flung skyward amid an almost deafening roar and clouds of steam from the catapult track. Seconds later, another aircraft will move into position and wait to be hurled into the sky.

With afterburners blazing, an F-14 Tomcat is catapulted from the bow of an aircraft carrier.

Each catapult is able to accelerate a fighter like the Grumman F-14 Tomcat from a standstill to a speed of 170 mph in a distance of just 90 yards. The gravity or G-force involved means that naval pilots must be superbly fit in order to cope with the stresses and strains that they face every day.

Landing on a carrier is much more dangerous than landing at an ordinary airfield. The carrier's flight deck is much shorter and much narrower than a normal runway. It can also move up and down a great deal, especially if a storm is blowing. Between them, these factors call for very precise flying. But there are some special aids that help the pilot to bring an aircraft aboard safely. Since the landing area is not much more than 150 yards long, it is not

A Hawkeye radar plane trails its hook moments before snagging an arrester wire.

possible for aircraft to stop by themselves. To allow them to land safely, they rely on arrester wires that catch a hook hanging below the aircraft.

Usually, pilots prefer to remain in control when trying to land at sea, but they can perform "hands-off" fully-automatic landings in the very worst weather, when visibility is nil. A computer makes this possible. Using data from several sources, it issues signals to an "automatic pilot," which is able to fly the aircraft during the critical approach and landing phase. It is hardly surprising that most pilots suffer from some anxiety during "hands-off" automatic

Helicopters and aircraft are both to be found on carriers like the USS *Forrestal*.

landings, for they are unable to see the ship until almost the moment of touchdown.

At the present time, all pilots who might have to fly in combat are men, but there are some women who do regularly operate to and from the big aircraft carriers. They pilot the twin-engined Grumman Grayhound transport aircraft, which are used to carry items such as mail and spare parts from shore bases out to the ships at sea. It might perhaps lack the glamour of flying fighter and attack aircraft, but it is a most important job. These women pilots may be succeeded by others who do have a combat role to fulfill.

Flying at sea does have its drawbacks. Ultimately, though, there is no shortage of applicants prepared to put up with the difficulties, for the sea-going life offers plenty of chances to see the world. Finally, there is the flying, which is among the best there is – very demanding as well as very rewarding.

Danger Facts

- Loss of steam power on launch can result in a "cold shot." This is when the aircraft falls into the sea due to lack of flying speed.

- Aircraft carriers always have a rescue helicopter airborne during flight operations, in case a plane crashes into the sea.

- Pilots select full power on landing so they can go around again if the hook fails to catch a wire or if the wire breaks.

GLOSSARY

Aerodynamics   Physical laws relating to flight.

Altitude   The vertical height of an object above sea level.

Arrester wires   Wires that slow down airplanes as they land on an aircraft carrier.

Civil   Non-military.

Cosmonaut   The Soviet term for someone who has flown into space.

Crop-dusting   A technique of flying low to spray special chemicals, such as insecticides, onto plants.

Forced landing   An emergency landing due to a sudden problem such as engine failure.

Formation flying   Two or more aircraft flying very close to each other and maneuvering as one. Aerobatic teams like the American Thunderbirds and Blue Angels, Australia's Roulettes, Canada's Snowbirds, and Britain's Red Arrows are experts.

G-force   Term relating to gravity pull. As this increases, the pilot's body feels heavier.

Interceptor   A fast fighter plane used to intercept enemy aircraft.

Mach One   The speed at which sound travels, typically around 733 mph.

Navigator   A person who directs a plane along a fixed route.

Solo   A term relating to a student's first flight without an instructor. It is usually limited to one circuit of the airfield.

Sound barrier   The speed of sound. Breaking the sound barrier involves flying faster than Mach One.

Squadron   A group of airplanes.

Stealth   A class of warplane specially designed to be almost invisible to radar.

Strike fighter   A warplane specially designed to attack targets with bombs or missiles.

Turbulence   Disturbed air that can result in a rough ride. It may be caused by storm activity or by events like forest fires.

Visibility   The clearness with which things can be seen.

INDEX

The numbers in **bold** refer to captions.